50 Mug Cake Recipes
Speedy Recipes for a Speedy Lifestyle

Copyright © 2015, Susan Tine

All rights Reserved. No part of this publication or the information in it may be quoted , from or reproduced in any form by means such as printing, scanning, photocopying or otherwise without prior written permission of the copyright holder.

Disclaimer and Terms of Use:

Effort has been made to ensure that the information in this book is accurate and complete, however, the author and the publisher do not warrant the accuracy of the information, text and graphics contained within the book due to the rapidly changing nature of science, research, known and unknown facts and internet. The Author and the publisher do not hold any responsibility for errors, omissions or contrary interpretation of the subject matter herein. This book is presented solely for motivational and informational purposes only.

Table of Contents

Table of Contents 3
Introduction 6
Strawberry in a Cup 7
Chocolate Mug Cake 8
Pumpkin Cake in Magic Mug 9
Apricot Cobbler in a Mug 10
Fruity Cream Cake in a Cup 11
French Toast Baked in a Mug 12
Chocolate Peanut Butter Miracle in Cup 13
Chocolate-Salted Caramel Cobbler 14
Gluten-Free Brownie in a Mug 15
Mango-Pineapple Cobbler in a Mug 16
Chocolate Gooey Cake in a Cup 17
Chocolate-Mallows Cake in a Cup 18
Mug Cake with Nutella Mix 19
A Sweet Cup of Potato Cake 20
Protein Mug Cake with German Chocolate Spice 21
Kiwi-Strawberry Cobbler in a Mug 22
Cream Cheese Frosted Cinnamon Cake 23
Fun-filled Cupcake 25
Nutella Oatmeal Cake in a Cup 26
Paleo Cake in a Cup 27

Low-Carb and Gluten Free Almond-Banana Cake ...28
Fruit Cocktail Cobbler in a Mug 29
Peanut Butter Cake with Frosting (sugar-free, gluten-free) 30
Mug Cake with Avocado Mix 31
Cherry-Nuts Tart in a Cup (High Protein) 32
Strawberry Shortcake in a Cup 33
Triple Chocolate Treat 34
Blueberry Gluten-Free Cheesecake 35
Confetti Party Mug Cake 36
Chocolate Espresso Mug Treat 37
Strawberry Vanilla Cake with Buttercream Glaze 38
Special Banana Cake in a Cup 40
Coconut Mug Cake with Lime Twist 41
Milk Chocolate Mug Cake Surprise 42
Mug Cake with Oreo Delight 43
Berry Mug Cake Spectacle 44
Coffee with Pumpkin Streusel Delight 45
Apple Pie Magic Mug 47
Banana Cake Frost with Cream Cheese Surprise 48
Cinnamon Cake Twist in a Cup 50
Chocolate Fudge with S'mores Sprinkles Mug Cake 51
Banana Mug Cake with Cinnamon Chips 52
Peach Cobbler in a Mug 53

Choco-Peanut Mug Cake 54
Blackberry and Blueberry Cobbler in a Mug..............55
The Red Velvet Thrill..56
Banana Strawberry Cobbler in a Mug 57
A Cup of Green Tea Mochi..58
Pumpkin with Caramel Twist 59
Pineapple Cobbler in a Mug 60
Conclusion 61

Introduction

Mug cakes are really easy to make, plus it is also delicious. Commonly, when making cakes in a mug you would need a microwave safe mug and a microwave to create one serving sized cakes. This way, it is faster to cook and cheaper to make especially if you live by yourself. Furthermore, making cakes in a mug also ensures that it's just good for one person and no additional servings can be had—unless of course you make another batch. This is especially helpful if you are watching your weight while still enjoying dessert.

When it comes to cooking mug cakes, always follow microwaving instructions. Basically, mug cakes are microwaved on high for at least a minute and then in intervals of 15 seconds or 30 seconds. This means that, after microwaving for a minute, you need to check your cake in a mug. Then, return the mug back into the microwave and cook for 15 or 30 seconds and then check your cake again. If you continuously microwave the cake without checking chances are the batter might overflow from the mug or you may overcook your cake—either way it is not good.

I hope you will enjoy these 50 differing mug cake recipes that I have in store for you.

Strawberry in a Cup

Ingredients:
2 tbsp milk
1 tbs butter
½ tsp baking powder
1 tbs white sugar
1/3 cup of flour
¼ cup powdered sugar
¾ cup strawberries

Directions:

1) In a mug, add powdered sugar and strawberries then stir to combine.
2) Mix all the remaining ingredients in a separate bowl.
3) On top of the strawberries, add the dough.
4) Microwave for about 1 ½ to 2 minutes then allow to cool-off.

Chocolate Mug Cake

Ingredients:
3-4 tbsp of mini chocolate chips
1 tbs of softened butter
1/3 cup of flour
3 tbsp of brown sugar
1 large egg

Directions:

1) In a microwavable mug, mix all ingredients thoroughly.
2) Microwave your cake for about 1.5 to 2 minutes.
3) You may also add a scoop of ice cream on top for additional flavor.

Pumpkin Cake in Magic Mug

Ingredients:
¼ tsp kosher salt
¼ tsp allspice
¼ tsp ground cinnamon
¼ cup brown sugar
7 tbsp all-purpose flour
¼ cup pumpkin puree
¼ tsp pure vanilla extract
2 tbsp skim milk
1 large egg

Directions:

1) Mix together all nine (9) ingredients in a bowl.
2) After mixing all ingredients, pour them in a microwavable mug and heat for about 3 minutes.
3) Enjoy!

Apricot Cobbler in a Mug

Ingredients:
3 tbsp white cake mix
A pinch or two of cinnamon
1 tbsp butter
2 ½ tbsp milk
1 4-oz can diced apricots
Scoop of ice cream – optional

Directions:

1) Melt butter in microwave safe small bowl.
2) In a microwave safe mug, mix well white cake mix, cinnamon, and milk.
3) Once done mixing, pour melted butter on top of batter and DO NOT mix.
4) For the apricots, reserve 2 tbsp of the liquid and drain apricot well. Top batter with apricots and pop in the oven for 1 ½ minutes.
5) Check if batter is cooked and if needed microwave in 30-second bursts.
6) Once cobbler is cooked, drizzle with reserved liquid, top with a scoop of ice cream if desired, and enjoy while hot.

Fruity Cream Cake in a Cup

Ingredients:
¼ cup fresh sliced strawberries
¼ cup whipped cream
5 tbsp all-purpose flour
4 tbsp granulated sugar
1/8 tsp vanilla extract
1/8 tsp baking powder
1 tbs vegetable oil
2 tbsp well-stirred strawberry yogurt
1 large egg

Directions:

1) Using a cooking spray, grease the inside of the mug then set aside.
2) Mix all ingredients in a bowl except for the strawberries and whipped cream.
3) Pour the mixture halfway full in the mug then microwave for 3 to 4 minutes.
4) Once baked, add whipped cream and strawberries.

French Toast Baked in a Mug

Ingredients:
3 tbsp milk
Pinch cinnamon
Drop of vanilla extract
1 large egg
1-2 pcs of any bread (your preference: white, croissant, wheat, multigrain)

Directions:

1) Slice bread in cubes.
2) Coat the inside of the mug with butter.
3) Fill mug with bread cubes
4) In a separate container, add a pinch of cinnamon, 3 tablespoons of milk, drop of vanilla extract and egg. Then, mix them all together.
5) Pour mixture down into your cup of bread. Allow it to soak down into the bread for about a minute.
6) Microwave between 1 to 2 minutes then add whip cream or syrup depending on your liking.

Chocolate Peanut Butter Miracle in Cup

Ingredients:
a small handful of chocolate chips
¼ tsp baking powder
1 tbsp cocoa
1 tbsp flour
2 tbsp peanut butter
1 tbsp brown sugar
1 egg

Directions:

1) Mix all ingredients in a bowl.
2) Coat your mug with butter and pour all mixture.
3) Microwave for 1-2 minutes.

Chocolate-Salted Caramel Cobbler

Ingredients:
2 salted caramels
1 tbsp vegetable oil
3 tbsp skim milk
1 egg – beaten
¼ tsp salt
¼ tsp baking powder
3 tbsp unsweetened cocoa powder
4 tbsp sugar
4 tbsp all-purpose flour

Directions:

1) Mix all ingredients in a small bowl excluding the salted caramels.
2) In a regular cup, pour in all mixture then sprinkle salted caramels on top of the mixture.
3) Microwave on high for about 1 to 2 minutes.

Gluten-Free Brownie in a Mug

Ingredients:
2 tbsp milk. Coffee or water
2 tbsp canola or other mild vegetable oil
Pinch salt
2 tbsp unsweetened cocoa powder
¼ cup packed brown sugar
¼ cup gluten-free oat flour, quinoa flour, or a gluten-free flour blend

Directions:

1) Mix salt, cocoa powder, brown sugar and gluten-free oat flour in a ramekin or mug. Thoroughly stir all ingredients to avoid lumps.
2) Add milk and oil to create thick paste.
3) For 1-2 minutes, microwave on high to achieve a springy but gooey brownie.

Mango-Pineapple Cobbler in a Mug

Ingredients:
3 tbsp white cake mix
A pinch or two of cinnamon
1 tbsp butter
2 ½ tbsp milk
2 tbsp mango puree
3 tbsp pineapple chunks, chopped
Scoop of ice cream – optional

Directions:

1) Melt butter in microwave safe small bowl.
2) In a microwave safe mug, mix well white cake mix, cinnamon, and milk.
3) Once done mixing, pour melted butter on top of batter and DO NOT mix.
4) Top batter with pineapple and pop in the oven for 1 ½ minutes.
5) Check if batter is cooked and if needed microwave in 30-second bursts.
6) Once cobbler is cooked, drizzle with mango puree, top with a scoop of ice cream if desired, and enjoy while hot.

Chocolate Gooey Cake in a Cup

Ingredients:
1 scoop ice cream
½ cup powdered sugar
¼ cup cocoa powder
1 egg

Directions:

1) Pour in all ingredients in a microwavable mug. Stir them altogether to form a batter.
2) Microwave for about 1 to 1 ½ minutes then add a scoop of ice cream on top.
3) Happy eating!

Chocolate-Mallows Cake in a Cup

Ingredients:
Marshmallow fluff for topping
1 egg
3 tbsp milk
3 tbsp peanut butter
33 tbsp melted butter
3 tbsp cocoa powder
4 tbsp self-rising flour
4 tbsp white sugar

Directions:

1) Mix all ingredients in a large cup and stir very well.
2) Microwave cup on high 1 ½ up to 3 minutes. Check the gooeyness of the cake using a toothpick.
3) Add the marshmallow fluff on top.

Mug Cake with Nutella Mix

Ingredients:
3 tbsp olive or vegetable oil
3 tbsp milk
3 tbsp Nutella
3 tbsp cocoa powder
1 egg
4 tbsp white granulated sugar
4 tbsp self-rising flour

Directions:

1) In a large mug, mix all ingredients. Stir well to form batter or until it becomes smooth.
2) For about 1.5 to 3 minutes, microwave mug.
3) Add chocolate syrup or whipped cream, which ever you desire.
4) Enjoy!

A Sweet Cup of Potato Cake

Ingredients:
3 tbsp toasted pecans or walnuts (chopped-optional)
½ tsp ground ginger
½ tsp freshly grated nutmeg
½ tsp ground cinnamon
Pinch of kosher salt
7 tbsp self-rising flour
¼ cup packed brown sugar
¼ tsp pure vanilla extract
2 tbsp soy, rice or almond milk
¼ cup mashed cooked sweet potatoes or sweet potato baby food
¼ cup water
1 tbsp egg substitute (like ground flax seeds)

Directions:

1) Stir water and egg substitute in a large mug. Leave for 5 minutes to thicken.
2) After 5 minutes, add all remaining ingredients.
3) Microwave for 1 ½ to 2 ½ minutes.

Protein Mug Cake with German Chocolate Spice

Ingredients:
1 tbsp coconut palm sugar
1/8 tsp baking soda
1/8 tsp baking powder
1.5 tbsp cocoa powder
1 tbsp fuel-6 chocolate protein powder
2 tbsp whole-wheat flour
4 tbsp almond milk, unsweetened
1 tsp coconut oil
1 large egg white

Directions:

1) Mix all ingredients in a medium-sized bowl
2) Coat mug with coconut oil and pour all mixtures.
3) Microwave on high for about 1 minute.

Kiwi-Strawberry Cobbler in a Mug

Ingredients:
3 tbsp white cake mix
A pinch or two of cinnamon
1 tbsp butter
2 ½ tbsp milk
2 kiwi fruit, peeled and pureed
3 medium strawberry, hulled and sliced
Scoop of ice cream – optional

Directions:

1) Melt butter in microwave safe small bowl.
2) In a microwave safe mug, mix well white cake mix, cinnamon, and milk.
3) Once done mixing, pour melted butter on top of batter and DO NOT mix.
4) Top batter with sliced strawberries and pop in the oven for 1 ½ minutes.
5) Check if batter is cooked and if needed microwave in 30-second bursts.
6) Once cobbler is cooked, drizzle with pureed kiwi, top with a scoop of ice cream if desired, and enjoy while hot.

Cream Cheese Frosted Cinnamon Cake

Cake Ingredients:
1 recipe cream cheese icing (view recipe below)
1/8 tsp (scant) salt
¼ tsp baking powder
1 dash ground nutmeg (optional)
¾ tsp ground cinnamon
2 ½ tbsp. Packed light-brown sugar
¼ cup + tbsp all-purpose flour
¼ tsp vanilla extract
1 tbsp buttermilk
1 tbsp vegetable oil
2 tbsp applesauce

Cream Cheese Icing Ingredients:
1 tsp milk
2 tbsp powdered sugar
1 tbsp cream cheese or Neufchatel cheese, softened

Directions:

1) Work on the cream cheese icing according to the given instructions then set aside.
2) Mix all other ingredients in a mug.
3) For about a minute, microwave mug and check if cake is fully cooked. You could add another 15 seconds if the cake needs to be cooked further.

4) Top cream cheese icing once done.

Directions for Cream Cheese Icing:

1) Mix all ingredients in a bowl until it smoothens.

Fun-filled Cupcake

Ingredients:
Sweetener (try 1 tbsp sugar or 1 packet stevia. If you use liquid sweetener, cut back on the other liquid.)
2 tsps sprinkles (or more or less as desired0
¼ tsp baking powder
¼ tsp vanilla extract
1 tbsp plus 1 tsp liquid (milk of choice or water)
1 tbsp applesauce, oil, pre-melted vegan butter or a combo (try coconut oil)
Heaping 1/16th tsp salt
3 tbsp flour (1.05oz) (see directions for flour notes)

Directions:

1) Pre-heat oven to 330 °F (165 °C).
2) Combine all ingredients and pour into a muffin pan sprayed or covered with oil.
3) Bake or cook for about 12 to 15 minutes. You may also cook this using a microwave, cook for 1.5 minutes and if needed cook for 30-second intervals until cooked to desired doneness.

Notes for Flour: You may use spelt flour or use white flour, whole-wheat pastry, or even Arrowhead Mills gluten-free. In case you've never done fat-free baking, you may use applesauce instead of oil in the recipe. This will still be yummy but gummier or denser than the regular cupcakes with oil.

Nutella Oatmeal Cake in a Cup

Ingredients:
1 tbsp Nutella or any chocolate-hazelnut spread, plus more to garnish
Pich nutmeg, optional
¼ tsp cinnamon, optional
1/8 tsp salt
¼ tsp baking powder
1 tbsp finely chopped pecans, plus more to garnish
1 ½ tbsp rolled oats
3 tbsp flour
1 tbsp sugar
1 tbsp olive oil
3 tbsp milk

Directions:

1) Combine sugar, olive oil and milk in a 12-ounce mug.
2) Mix all remaining ingredients except for the Nutella.
3) Top Nutella and gently push downward in order to be partially mixed in the cake batter.
4) For 30 seconds microwave on high and check if cake looks dry and cooked. You made add additional 15 seconds based your desired doneness.
5) Once done, leave cake for about 5 minutes then you may add more Nutella if desired.

Paleo Cake in a Cup

Ingredients:
1 tbsp vanilla
2 tbsp maple syrup
2 tbsp chocolate chips (you may use enjoy Life Chocolate Chips since they are gluten, soy and dairy free)
1 tbsp almond flour
1 tbsp coconut flour
1 large egg

Directions:

1) Mix well all ingredients in your mug.
2) Microwave your mug for about 1 to 1½ minutes then enjoy your cake!

Low-Carb and Gluten Free Almond-Banana Cake

Ingredients:
1 tbsp coconut flour
Pinch of salt
1 1/2 tsp vanilla extract
½ tsp baking powder
1 egg
1 tbsp almond butter
1/3 cup almond flour
1/3 cup mashed ripe banana
2 tbsp butter

Directions:

1) In a medium-sized bowl, melt butter then add all other ingredients.
2) Transfer mixture to 4 greased paper baking cups then place cups on a microwavable plate.
3) Microwave for about 1 to 1 ½ minutes then serve banana slices on top.

Fruit Cocktail Cobbler in a Mug

Ingredients:
3 tbsp white cake mix
A pinch or two of cinnamon
1 tbsp butter
2 ½ tbsp milk
¼ cup fruit cocktail, drained and reserving 2 tbsp juice
Scoop of ice cream – optional

Directions:

1) Melt butter in microwave safe small bowl.
2) In a microwave safe mug, mix well white cake mix, cinnamon, and milk.
3) Once done mixing, pour melted butter on top of batter and DO NOT mix.
4) For the fruit cocktail, reserve 2 tbsp of the liquid and drain fruit cocktail well. Top batter with fruit cocktail and pop in the oven for 1 ½ minutes.
5) Check if batter is cooked. If needed, microwave in 30-second bursts.
6) Once cobbler is cooked, drizzle with reserved liquid, top with a scoop of ice cream if desired, and enjoy while hot.

Peanut Butter Cake with Frosting (sugar-free, gluten-free)

Ingredients:
1 tsp baking powder
¼ cup peanut flour
¼ cup oat flour
1/8 tsp salt
4 packets Truvia
¼ cup unsweetened applesauce
1/3 cup unsweetened vanilla almond milk
1 tbsp ground flaxseed

Directions:

1) Grease a 4 inches of baking dish.
2) Mix all ingredients in a medium-sized bowl. Ensure that you mix well so that there are no clumps.
3) Pour mixture or batter into the baking dish
4) Bake thru a microwave for about 6 minutes. Once the cake is springy then it is done or ready to serve.

Mug Cake with Avocado Mix

Ingredients:
5 tbsp fat-free milk
3 tbsp mashed avocado (close to half of a medium avocado)
¼ tsp baking powder
4 ½ tbsp. Sugar
4 tbsp flour

Directions:

1) Mix all ingredients in a large mug. Ensure batter is smooth.
2) Microwave for about 2 minutes. Use toothpick to determine if cake is no longer wet. Once clean, then it is done already.
3) Enjoy!

Cherry-Nuts Tart in a Cup (High Protein)

Ingredients:
Garnish: whipped cream, Greek-style yogurt or ice cream
5 frozen tart cherries
Dash of grated orange zests
Dash of salt
2 tsps honey
1 tbsp unsweetened almond butter
3 tbsp milk
1 tbsp vanilla whey protein powder
2 tbsp powdered peanut butter

Directions:

1) Combine all ingredients except for the tart cherries.
2) Grease mug with cooking spray and pour all mixtures then top cherries into batter.
3) For about 1 ½ to 2 minutes, microwave on high.
4) Add yogurt or ice cream on top.

Strawberry Shortcake in a Cup

Ingredients:
Pinch of salt
1/8 tsp baking soda
½ cup flour
½ tsp vanilla
1 egg
¼ cup vegetable oil
1.2 cup buttermilk
½ cup sugar
1 chopped strawberry
1 tbsp white chocolate chips

Directions:

1) Cover with butter 4 small microwave-safe mugs.
2) Mix all ingredients in a bowl except for the berries and chocolate chips.
3) Add chopped strawberry and white chocolate chips into each mug and pour out 1/3 cup batter in every mug.
4) Set microwave for 2 minutes then check cake if done thru using a toothpick. Once it comes out clean then it is done.
5) Let it cool and top with more strawberries as desired.

Triple Chocolate Treat

Ingredients:
Pinch of salt
1/8 tsp baking soda
1/3 cup flour
½ tsp vanilla
1 egg
¼ cup vegetable oil
1.2 cup buttermilk
½ cup sugar
2 tbsp Dutch-process cocoa powder

Directions:

1) Cover with butter 4 small microwave-safe mugs.
2) Mix all ingredients in a bowl and pour out 1/3 cup batter in every mug.
3) Set microwave for 2 minutes then check cake if done thru using a toothpick. Once it comes out clean then it is done.
4) Let it cool and add chocolate sprinkles or chocolate ice cream.

Blueberry Gluten-Free Cheesecake

Ingredients:
1 tsp dried blueberries
Pinch of salt
1 tsp vanilla
1 tsp lemon juice
2 tbsp cornstarch
¼ cup confectioner's sugar (should be gluten-free)
1 large egg
8 ounces cream cheese

Directions:

1) Grease 4 small microwave-safe mugs with butter.
2) About 30 seconds, microwave the 8 ounces of cream cheese in a bowl.
3) Mix all ingredients in the bowl with the melted cream cheese.
4) In each mug, pour out ¼ cup batter and mix dried berries into each.
5) Set microwave for 2 minutes (one mug at a time) then check cake if done using a toothpick. Once it comes out clean then it is done. An additional 15 seconds can be added to the time if needed.
6) Let it cool and add more berries as desired.

Confetti Party Mug Cake

Ingredients:
Pinch of salt
1/8 tsp baking soda
1/3 cup flour
½ tsp vanilla
1 egg
¼ cup vegetable oil
1.2 cup buttermilk
½ cup sugar
2 tsps rainbow sprinkles

Directions:

1) Cover 4 small microwave-safe mugs with butter.
2) Mix all ingredients in a bowl except for the rainbow sprinkles.
3) Add rainbow sprinkles in each mug then pour out 1/3 cup batter in each.
4) Set microwave for 2 minutes then check cake if done thru using a toothpick. Once it comes out clean then it is done.
5) Let it cool and add whipped cream and more rainbow sprinkles.

Chocolate Espresso Mug Treat

Ingredients:
½ tsp vanilla extract
2 tbsp oil
1 large egg
2 tbsp milk
¼ tsp baking powder
2 ½ to 3 tbsp sugar
2 tbsp drinking chocolate powder or sweetened cocoa powder
1 tsp instant coffee powder
3 tbsp all-purpose flour

Directions:

1) Combine all ingredients in a bowl and mix well.
2) Pour batter into a coated or greased mug.
3) Microwave on high for about 1 to 2 minutes then top with vanilla ice cream.

Strawberry Vanilla Cake with Buttercream Glaze

Ingredients:
2-3 tbsp diced strawberries
½ tsp baking powder
¼ cup all-purpose flour
2-3 tbsp granulated sugar
½ tsp vanilla extract
1 large egg
1 tbsp butter, softened

Vanilla Buttercream Glaze
1 tbsp cream or milk
¼ tsp vanilla extract (or ½ tsp vanilla)
¼ cup powdered sugar
1 tbsp melted butter

Directions:

1) Grease a large mug with cooking spray.
2) Mix all ingredients in a bowl except for the strawberries. Mix well until batter is smooth.
3) Pour batter into mug. If there is extra batter you may bake 2 mug cakes.
4) Microwave for 1 to 2 minutes but check cake using a toothpick to determine its doneness.
5) Let it cool then create the glaze by combining all ingredients in another bowl except for the cream or milk.

6) Slowly add cream depending on your desired thickness of the glaze.
7) Before adding glaze on to mug cake, top cake with diced strawberries and then add glaze over mug cake and strawberries. Allow glaze to soak into the cake.

Special Banana Cake in a Cup

Ingredients:
1 scoop of coffee ice cream
½ tsp baking powder
3 tbsp brown sugar
3 tbsp plain flour
1 ripe banana (mashed)
1 tbsp milk
1 egg (lightly beaten)
1 tbsp butter, melted (or flavorless oil)

Directions:

1) Melt butter into the mug by microwaving it for 10 seconds.
2) Add milk and then lightly beat the egg to combine with milk.
3) Mix all remaining ingredients except the ice cream.
4) Microwave mug in medium heat for about 1 minute. If the cake is still undercooked, cook it for about 10 more seconds. Once cooked, the mug cake should then rise and be gooey.
5) Top it off with a scoop of coffee ice cream.

Coconut Mug Cake with Lime Twist

Ingredients:
¼ tsp lime zest
1 tsp coconut flakes
4 tbsp full fat coconut milk
2 ½ tbsp Granulated sugar
¼ tsp baking powder
4 tbsp all-purpose flour

Directions:

1) Mix all ingredients in your mug except for the coconut flakes and lime zest.
2) Stir all components thoroughly to create a smooth batter. Ensure that no flour is sticking around the sides of the mug.
3) Garnish top of batter with coconut flakes.
4) For about a minute, microwave your mug then add lime zest on top.
5) Enjoy your mug cake with a lime twist!

Milk Chocolate Mug Cake Surprise

Ingredients:
Optional: 6-7 mini marshmallows
1 large marshmallow
2-3 small squares of milk chocolates
2 tbsp granulated sugar
3 tbsp fat free milk
1 tbsp vegetable oil
¼ tsp baking powder
2 tbsp finely crushed graham crackers
4 tbsp all-purpose flour

Directions:

1) Mix all ingredients in a microwave-safe mug except for the marshmallows. To avoid flour chunks make sure to mix well.
2) Once the batter is all smooth, make a hole in the middle and place the chocolate squares.
3) Microwave mug for about a minute, once top of the cake is dry and gooey, take it out.
4) Add mini marshmallows on top and heat again for 20 seconds. Then top it up with the large marshmallow.
5) Enjoy!

Mug Cake with Oreo Delight

Ingredients:
½ cup milk
½ tsp baking powder
9 Oreo cookies

Directions:

1) Mix the milk and the baking powder in a bowl.
2) In a separate bowl, crush all cookies.
3) Add cookies to the rest of the ingredients then mix thoroughly.
4) In a microwavable mug, pour in the batter and cook for 2 minutes.
5) Once done, top it off with a scoop of your favorite ice cream.

Berry Mug Cake Spectacle

Ingredients:
1 tbsp Almond milk or plain soy milk
Brown sugar
Small handful of blueberries
1 large egg
Quarter cup of quick oats

Directions:

1) Mix all ingredients in a microwavable-safe mug.
2) Once batter is smooth place in a microwave for about 1 to 2 minutes.
3) Enjoy!

Coffee with Pumpkin Streusel Delight

Ingredients:
Pinch of ground cloves
Pinch of salt
Few drops of vanilla extract
1/8 tsp baking powder
¼ tsp cinnamon
¼ cup self-rising flour
1 tbsp brown sugar
1 tbsp butter
2 tbsp sugar
2 tbsp flour
2 tbsp pumpkin puree

Directions:

1) Soften the butter for five seconds in a microwavable mug. Ensure that butter is not melted.
2) Mix the sugar thoroughly with the pumpkin puree, baking powder, pinch of salt, self-rising flour and few drops of vanilla.
3) In a separate container or bowl, mix with hands 2 tbsp flour, 1 tbsp butter, cinnamon and brown sugar to make a streusel.
4) Get your cake batter and pour your streusel on top.
5) Microwave mug for 1 ½ minutes.

6) Your Pumpkin Streusel Delight in a mug is best enjoyed with a cup of steaming hot coffee.

Apple Pie Magic Mug

Ingredients:
½ sheet of graham crackers (crumbled)
1 medium Fuji apple 9cut into ½-inch cubes
2 tbsp whipped cream
12 pcs cinnamon flavored candy
A dash of cinnamon

Directions:

1) Place candies and apple cubes in your mug and microwave for 2 minutes.
2) Remove mug and stir thoroughly then microwave again for a minute.
3) Once the apples are soft, let it cool for ten minutes.
4) Sprinkle graham crumbs then top it off with whipped cream then cinnamon.
5) Enjoy!

Banana Cake Frost with Cream Cheese Surprise

Ingredients:
1 tbsp applesauce
1 pinch salt
1 tbsp buttermilk
1 tbsp chopped walnuts or peanuts
1 tbsp vegetable oil
1 large egg yolk
Banana slices (optional)
½ cup all-purpose flour
¼ tsp baking powder
¼ tsp vanilla extract
1/8 tsp cinnamon
½ over-ripe banana (mashed well)

Ingredients for Cream Cheese Frosting:
1 and ½ tbsp softened cream cheese
4 tbsp powder sugar

Directions:

1) Pour the following ingredients in a microwavable mug and mix thoroughly: baking powder, sugar, flour, salt and cinnamon.
2) Add and blend well the vegetable oil, buttermilk, egg yolk, mashed banana and applesauce.
3) Microwave cake for about 2 ½ until 3 minutes.

4) In a separate bowl, combine all ingredients of cream cheese frosting.
5) Top of your cake with the frosting once done.

Cinnamon Cake Twist in a Cup

Ingredients:
¾ tsp cinnamon powder
¼ tsp baking powder
¼ tsp vanilla extract
¼ cup + 1 tbsp all-purpose flour
2 tbsp applesauce
2 ½ tbsp Packed light brown sugar
1/8 scant tsp salt
1 tbsp oil
1 dash nutmeg powder
1 tbsp buttermilk

Ingredients for the Frosting:
2 tbsp powdered sugar
1 tbsp cream cheese
1 tsp milk

Directions:

1) Thoroughly mix all the ingredients in your microwavable cup.
2) For 1 to ½ minutes, microwave cup.
3) Then, work on the frosting by mixing all the ingredients. Mix well to make frosting creamy and smooth.
4) Let your cake cool in few seconds then top if off with frosting.

Chocolate Fudge with S'mores Sprinkles Mug Cake

Ingredients:
Marshmallows
Pinch of Salt
1 large egg
1/8 tsp baking powder
3 tbsp graham cracker crumbs
3 ½ tbsp unsalted butter (melted)
¼ cup whole wheat pastry flour
½ tsp vanilla extract
1 ½ oz milk chocolate (chopped)
2 tbsp granulated sugar

Directions:

1) Mix 1 oz chocolate and 3 tbsps butter and microwave for 25 seconds.
2) On a separate small bowl, mix with hands remaining butter and graham crackers crumbs.
3) Then mix all other ingredients in another bowl.
4) Top off batter over graham crust then microwave for 1 minute and additional 20 seconds. You may extend it up to 2 minutes then top off with marshmallows.
5) Microwave the mug for another 10 seconds to melt the marshmallows.
6) Then it's ready to serve…Enjoy!

Banana Mug Cake with Cinnamon Chips

Ingredients:
2 tbsp over-ripe banana, mashed
½ tsp baking powder
3 ½ tbsp no-fat milk
4 tbsp self-rising flour
1 tbsp mini cinnamon chips
1/8 tsp cinnamon
2 tbsps granulated sugar

Directions:

1) Thoroughly whisk together mashed banana, sugar, baking powder, no-fat milk, flour and cinnamon in a microwave safe mug.
2) Once done mixing thoroughly, add half of the cinnamon chips into the mug and mix again.
3) Once ready to cook, sprinkle remaining cinnamon chips on top of batter and microwave for a minute.
4) If needed, microwave in 15 second burst until cooked to desired doneness.
5) Serve and enjoy.

Peach Cobbler in a Mug

Ingredients:
3 tbsp white cake mix
A pinch or two of cinnamon
1 tbsp butter
2 ½ tbsp milk
1 4-oz can diced peaches
Scoop of ice cream – optional

Directions:

1) Melt butter in microwave safe small bowl.
2) In a microwave safe mug, mix well white cake mix, cinnamon, and milk.
3) Once done mixing, pour melted butter on top of batter and DO NOT mix.
4) For the peaches, reserve 2 tbsp of the liquid and drain peaches well. Top batter with peaches and pop in the oven for 1 ½ minutes.
5) Check if batter is cooked and if needed microwave in 30-second bursts.
6) Once cobbler is cooked, drizzle with reserved liquid, top with a scoop of ice cream if desired, and enjoy while hot.

Choco-Peanut Mug Cake

Ingredients:
1 tbsp + 2 tsps cocoa powder
¼ tsp pure vanilla extract
3 tbsp powdered peanut butter
3 tbsp non-fat milk
A pinch of salt
2 tsps vegetable oil
1 tsp xylitol or sugar
1 tbsp stevia
¼ tsp baking powder

Directions:

1) Mix all ingredients thoroughly in a microwave safe mug.
2) Pop mug in the microwave and cook for a minute and 15 seconds.
3) Check cake if already done by inserting a toothpick in the middle. If batter sticks to toothpick, continue microwaving in 15-second bursts.
4) Once cooked to desired doneness, cool for at least 5 minutes and enjoy.

Blackberry and Blueberry Cobbler in a Mug

Ingredients:
3 tbsp white cake mix
A pinch or two of cinnamon
1 tbsp butter
2 ½ tbsp milk
2 tbsp blackberries
2 tbsp blueberries
Scoop of ice cream–optional

Directions:

1) Melt butter in microwave safe small bowl.
2) In a microwave safe mug, mix well white cake mix, cinnamon, and milk.
3) Once done mixing, pour melted butter on top of batter and DO NOT mix.
4) For the berries, chop berries reserve 2 tbsp of the liquid and drain berries well before placing on top of batter. Do not mix.
5) Pop in the microwave oven for 1 ½ minutes.
6) Check if batter is cooked and if needed, microwave in 30-second bursts.
7) Once done, pour reserved liquid on top of cobbler and top with a scoop of ice cream if desired and enjoy while hot.

The Red Velvet Thrill

Ingredients:
3 tbsp butter
3 tbsp buttermilk
4 tbsp self-rising flour
4 ½ tbsp Sugar
½ tsp red food coloring
1 ½ tbsp Unsweetened cocoa powder
1/8 tsp baking powder

Directions:

1) Melt butter around 10 to 15 seconds in a microwave safe mug.
2) Remove mug and mix all remaining ingredients. Make sure to stir or blend them thoroughly.
3) Ensure to press dough evenly down to the bottom of the mug.
4) Microwave for 50 to 70 seconds and let it cool, then ready to serve.

Banana Strawberry Cobbler in a Mug

Ingredients:
3 tbsp white cake mix
A pinch or two of cinnamon
1 tbsp butter
2 ½ tbsp milk
½ medium banana, sliced
3 medium strawberries, hulled and pureed
Scoop of ice cream – optional

Directions:

1) Melt butter in microwave safe small bowl.
2) In a microwave safe mug, mix well white cake mix, cinnamon, and milk.
3) Once done mixing, pour melted butter on top of batter and DO NOT mix.
4) Pop in the oven for 1 ½ minutes.
5) Check if batter is cooked and if needed, microwave in 30-second bursts.
6) Once cobbler is cooked, top with sliced banana and drizzle with pureed strawberries. If desired, top with a scoop of ice cream and enjoy while hot.

A Cup of Green Tea Mochi

Ingredients:
1 tsp high quality green tea powder
1 large egg
4 tbsp glutinous rice flour
4 tbsp sugar
¼ baking powder
5 tbsp milk

Directions:

1) Mix all ingredients in a bowl.
2) Once the batter is smooth, pour them into two mugs or cups.
3) Cook each mug separately at high for 90 to 110 seconds (1 minute and 30 seconds up to 1 minute and 50 seconds) then allow it to cool off.
4) Enjoy!

Pumpkin with Caramel Twist

Ingredients:
1 large egg
Caramel sauce
2 slices of bread (cubed)
2 heaping tbsp of pumpkin puree
1/8 tsp cinnamon
4 tbsp milk
2-3 tbsp sugar

Directions:

1) Put in the bread cubes at the bottom of microwave safe mug. You may use 2 mugs.
2) Blend all other ingredients well in a separate bowl then pour mixture into your mugs, so that all the bread pieces are coated with batter.
3) Microwave between 1 to 2 ½ minutes and top it with caramel sauce and ice cream of your choice.

Pineapple Cobbler in a Mug

Ingredients:
3 tbsp white cake mix
A pinch or two of cinnamon
1 tbsp butter
2 ½ tbsp milk
1 4-oz can diced pineapple
Scoop of ice cream – optional

Directions:

1) Melt butter in microwave safe small bowl.
2) In a microwave safe mug, mix well white cake mix, cinnamon and milk.
3) Once done mixing, pour melted butter on top of batter and DO NOT mix.
4) For the pineapple, reserve 2 tbsp of the liquid and drain pineapple well. Top batter with pineapple and pop in the oven for 1 ½ minutes.
5) Check if batter is cooked and if needed microwave in 30-second bursts.
6) Once cobbler is cooked, drizzle with reserved liquid, top with a scoop of ice cream if desired, and enjoy while hot.

Conclusion

Now that you have seen all the mug cake recipes I have prepared for you, I hope that you will try making all of them, as they are really delicious as well as they are easy to make. If you want to make your mug cakes uber special just add your favorite frosting or a scoop of ice cream on top and garnish with your favorite nuts. To make your mug cakes more interesting for kids, just add a dash of sprinkles or colored crystal sugars as accents.

I hope that you will enjoy these mug cake recipes for years to come.

Printed by Amazon Italia Logistica S.r.l.
Torrazza Piemonte (TO), Italy